AMERICAN SHORTHAIRS

MARYSA STORM

Black Rabbit Books

Bolt Jr. is published by Black Rabbit Books
P.O. Box 227, Mankato, Minnesota, 56002.
www.blackrabbitbooks.com
Copyright © 2025 Black Rabbit Books

Alissa Thielges, editor
Rhea Magaro, designer

All rights reserved. No part of this book may be reproduced in any form without written permission from the publisher.

Names: Storm, Marysa, author.
Title: American shorthairs / by Marysa Storm.
Description: Mankato, MN: Black Rabbit Books, [2025] | Series: Bolt Jr. Our favorite cats | Includes bibliographical references and index. | Audience: Ages 5–8 | Audience: Grades K–1
Identifiers: LCCN 2024010407 (print) | LCCN 2024010408 (ebook) | ISBN 9781644666777 (library binding) | ISBN 9781644666951 (ebook)
Subjects: LCSH: American shorthair cat—Juvenile literature.
Classification: LCC SF449.A45 S76 2025 (print) | LCC SF449.A45 (ebook) | DDC 636.8/2—dc23/eng/20240412
LC record available at https://lccn.loc.gov/2024010407
LC ebook record available at https://lccn.loc.gov/2024010408

Image Credits

Dreamstime/Slowmotiongli, 23; Shutterstock/A7880S, 14, ANURAK PONGPATIMET, 18, 20–21, ANUCHA PONGPATIMETH, 11, Cat Box, 1, Dmitrij Skorobogatov, cover, Eric Isselee, 7, Koumaru, 17, Paisit Teeraphatsakool, 21, pimlim, 12, Polina Tomtosova, 3, 24, Pony3000, 19, Puripat Lertpunyaroj, 4, 10, Robert Way, 5, RustezeDesigns, 6, Tom Wang, 13, Top Photo Engineer, 8–9

Contents

Chapter 1
Meet the American Shorthair 4

Chapter 2
Personality 10

Chapter 3
American Shorthair Care 16

More Information 22

CHAPTER 1
Meet the American Shorthair

With wide eyes, an American shorthair looks out a window. It's watching a bird. The cat dreams of leaping after it. Its hunting **instincts** make it want to pounce.

instinct: a natural feeling that is not learned and affects how you act or think

Strong Cats

American shorthairs were born to hunt. These powerful cats have strong muscles. They have big faces and short hair. They come in many colors. Silver is the most common.

▶ Maine Coon
8 to 18 pounds
(4 to 8 kg)

PARTS OF AN American Shorthair

strong legs

paws

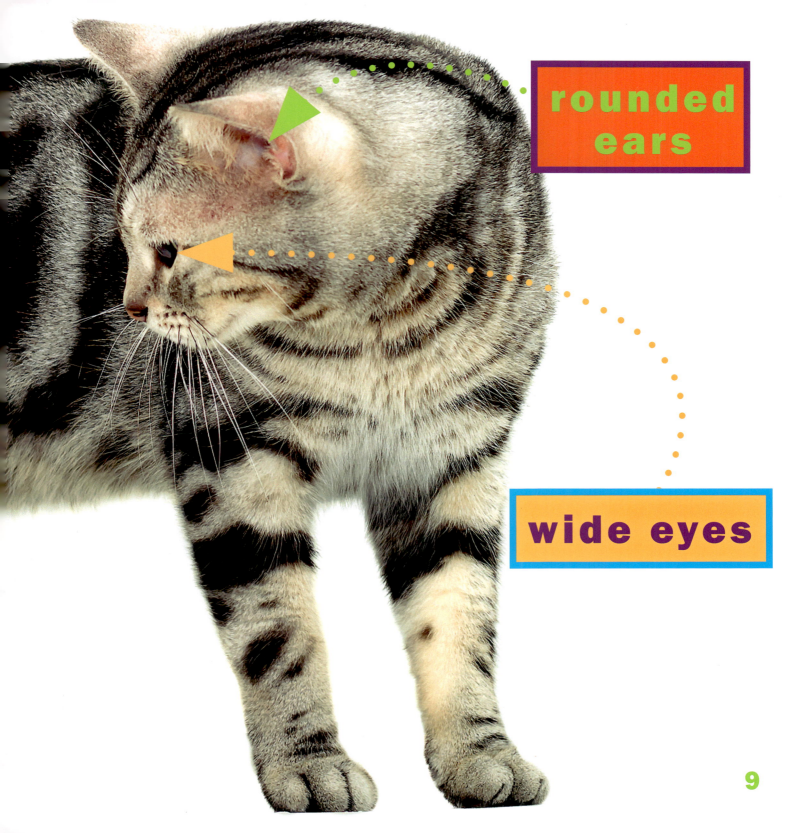

CHAPTER 2

Personality

American shorthairs enjoy hunting. They also like to play. They love **interactive** toys. These cats get along well with other cats and kids. They will play with nice dogs too.

interactive: acting with each other

FACT

Shorthairs play well by themselves.

11

Cuddling and Chirping

American shorthairs will cuddle with their owners when they want. But they also like curling up in sunny spots alone. These cats are quiet. If they need something, they'll **chirp**.

chirp: a short, sharp sound

An Old History

Shorthairs traveled to the United States on ships.

United States

CHAPTER 3

American Shorthair Care

American shorthairs need care. Weekly brushing keeps their coats shiny. Owners should not overfeed these cats. Otherwise, they may become overweight. These cats need exercise too. Owners should play with them every day.

FACT

Cat nails should be trimmed about twice a month.

Friendly Felines

Owners love their American shorthairs. The cats are easy to take care of. They make sweet friends too. It is no wonder they are popular cats!

American Shorthair's Height
8 to 10 inches
(20 to 25 centimeters)

Bonus Facts

Their eyes are green or gold.

Most American shorthairs don't like being carried.

They live 15 to 20 years.

The breed was first called the **domestic shorthair.**

domestic: living near or with humans

21

READ MORE/WEBSITES

Burling, Alexis. *Cats.* Minneapolis: Abdo Publishing Company, 2024.

Noelle, Becky. *American Shorthair.* New York: Lightbox Learning Inc., 2024.

Woodson, Cameron L. *American Shorthairs.* Minneapolis: Jump!, 2021.

American Shorthair
kids.britannica.com/students/article/American-shorthair/309825

American Shorthair Cat Breed
cats.com/cat-breeds/american-shorthair

American Shorthair Facts for Kids
kids.kiddle.co/American_Shorthair

GLOSSARY

instinct (IN-stingkt)—a natural feeling that is not learned and affects how you act or think

interactive (in-ter-AK-tiv)—acting with each other

chirp (CHURP)—a short, sharp sound

domestic (duh-MES-tik)—living near or with humans

INDEX

B
body parts, 4, 7, 8–9, 20

C
care, 16, 19
colors, 7

L
life span, 20

O
origins, 14–15

P
personality, 4, 7, 10, 13, 19

S
sizes, 6–7, 19
sounds, 13

T
toys, 10